Featherstone

# 50

## fantastic ideas for
# creativity outdoors

ALISTAIR BRYCE-CLEGG

Published 2013 by Featherstone Education
an imprint of Bloomsbury Publishing plc
50 Bedford Square, London, WC1B 3DP
**www.bloomsbury.com**

ISBN 978-1-4081-8677-0

Printed and bound in India by Replika Press Pvt Ltd

This book is produced using paper that is made from wood grown in
managed, sustainable forests. It is natural, renewable and recyclable.
The logging and manufacturing processes conform to the environmental
regulations of the country of origin.

10  9  8  7  6  5  4  3

To see our full range of titles visit **www.bloomsbury.com**

**Acknowledgements**
We would like to thank the staff and children of the following settings for their time
and patience in helping put this book together, including the use of a number of
photographs:

London Early Years Foundation, Emli Bendixen
Noah's Ark Pre-School
Edmondsley Primary School
Thomas More Roman Catholic Primary School
Woodhouse Community Primary School
The Arches Primary School
Cosy Foundation (Cosy Direct)

Also special thanks to Fee Bryce-Clegg & Kirstine Beeley

# Contents

# Introduction

The outdoors is an amazing place to teach and learn. You will find that it is never the same two days in a row. Something is always changing – from the flowers that are blooming to the different shapes of the clouds in the sky. There is always something new to look at and creativity to take inspiration from.

Outside is a place where children love to be active, to run and jump and play at a fast pace. Sometimes they have to be reminded or encouraged to stop and take a closer look at a space that they might once have thought they were very familiar with. You will be amazed at how much awe and wonder there can be in the simplest and smallest of outdoor spaces.

There is no better place for children to learn about colour, pattern, shape and texture than the outdoors. Here the children can see, hear, smell and touch these things first hand, their discoveries inspiring them to make creations of their own.

Children are naturally inquisitive and love to experiment and explore. For them, touch is a very powerful means of finding out about how something is made and how it works. You will find that children are far more likely to use something in their play if they have been part of creating it. Lots of the activities in this book have been specifically chosen so that children can be involved in their creation from the start. I have tried to include as many creative dimensions to the activities as I can. The more senses that are engaged in any activity, the more powerful the learning experience will be for the children.

In this book I have attempted to include a range of activities, some that only involve the use of the natural environment and some that take their inspiration from Mother Nature as a springboard to the creation of other things. An important feature of all of the activities is that there are lots of opportunities for children to talk about what they are discovering and what they think about it. The activities need to be meaningful and appropriate to the children's stage development rather than an 'everyone make one of these' approach.

Sometimes you will end up completing the activity you started but often you might find that children take their learning in a completely different direction, which is great! What I hope I have given you is 50 starting points or 50 ideas to get children thinking and exploring. How the activities turn out could be different every time you try them!

So get your wellies on, get outside and get creative!

50 Fantastic Ideas for Creativity Outdoo

## Skin allergy alert

Some detergents and soaps
can cause skin reactions.
Always be mindful of potential skin allergies
when letting children mix anything with
their hands and always provide lots of
facilities to wash materials off after they
have been in contact with the skin. Watch
out for this symbol on the relevant pages.

## Food allergy alert

When using food stuffs
to enhance the activities
always be mindful of potential food
allergies. We have used this symbol on
the relevant pages.

## What you need:

- Cardboard tube
- Greaseproof paper
- Duct tape
- Scissors
- 1½ cups of plaster of Paris
- 3 tablespoons of powder paint
- ¾ cup of warm water

## What to do:

1. Line the inside of your tube with greaseproof paper.
2. Stick strips of duct tape across the bottom of one end of the tube to seal it.
3. Mix the powder paint with the plaster of Paris.
4. Add the water and stir.
5. Pour the mixture into your lined tube.
6. Leave to harden (overnight).
7. When the mixture is dry, peel off the card and greaseproof paper and get drawing outside!

**Warning!**

Never pour excess plaster of Paris down the drain – it will block it!

### Taking it forward

- Make multi-coloured chalk by using more than one colour of the plaster of Paris mix in the same tube.
- Make mini versions by pouring your mixture into silicone moulds.
- Add a wrist strap by inserting one end of a loop of string or wool into the open end of the tube while the mixture is still wet.

### What's in it for the children?

Not only will the children be involved in all of the talk and discovery around the creation of their giant chalks, they will also have the opportunity to develop their gross and fine motor skills along with their artistic talents when using them.

# ardboard tube bird feeder

## What you need:

- Peanut butter *(check for nut allergies)*
- Cardboard tube
- Mixed bird seed or breakfast cereal
- Knife
- String

## What to do:

1. Cover the cardboard tube with the peanut butter using the knife.

2. Roll it in the bird seed or breakfast cereal.

3. Pierce two holes in the cardboard tube, thread the string through it and tie the ends together allowing enough space to be able to hang it from a tree!

**FOOD allergy !**

### king it forward

Try making feeding tubes of different sizes.

Try different coatings for the bird feeder and see which the birds like best.

Set up a bird watching station with binoculars.

Set up art and creative resources so that the children can recreate the birds that they see.

### nat's in it for the children?

e children will be able to engage the processes involved in the eation of their bird feeder. They will o have the opportunity to observe ds in detail and create artistic resentations of what they see.

### Top tip ⭐

f you are unable to use peanut outter then you can use a thick flour and water paste or fat ike lard.

*Health & Safety*

Ensure that the children are supervised at all times when knives are being used

# Balloon marbles

## What you need:

- Party balloons
- Water
- Food colouring
- Cotton buds
- Freezer

## What to do:

1. Fill the balloon with water.

2. When the balloon is full, add some food colouring using the cotton bud. Simply stick the cotton bud into the food colouring and then put it down the neck of the balloon and into the water. Alternatively you could use a syringe if you have got one.

3. Tie the balloon.

4. Leave in the freezer overnight.

5. When frozen remove from the freezer and remove the balloon from the ice.

6. Leave outside for discovery.

### Taking it forward

- Try making balloon marbles of different sizes.

- Add glitter to the water before you freeze it.

- Put small objects into the balloon before you freeze it for discovery later.

- Try doing the activity during winter and leave the balloons outside to freeze.

### What's in it for the children?

The children will get to experience how water can change to ice and then back to water again.

There are lots of opportunities for talk and discussion around the colours and shapes that the children will be able to see inside the ice marbles.

# Home made rain stick

## What you need:

- **Cardboard tube from a roll of wrapping paper** (or 3 kitchen roll tubes joined together)
- **Split pins**
- **Masking tape**
- **Rice, peas or beans** (uncooked)
- **Paint**

## What to do:

1. Rolls of cardboard usually have a spiral seam running down their length. Follow this seam pushing in a split pin every 2cm.
2. Once all of the split pins are in, cover the outside of the roll in masking tape.
3. Seal up one of the ends of the tube using masking tape.
4. Pour one cup of the rice, peas or beans into the open end of the tube.
5. Seal the open end with more masking tape.
6. Paint and decorate the outside of your tube.
7. Take outside and tip backwards and forwards to hear the rain.

### king it forward

For younger children with smaller hands you can make a shorter version from the inner tube of a toilet roll.

Research how dancing is used in some cultures to bring rain and create your own rain stick rain dance.

### at's in it for the children?

s is a great activity for not only veloping children's fine motor xterity but also their listening ls. In the making of their rain k they will also engage in lots of ls around colour, texture, pattern d design.

# Tin can drums

## What you need:

- Empty tin cans of various sizes

## What to do:

1. Wash your tins out thoroughly and ensure that there are no sharp edges.

2. Remove any labels.

3. Push the open end of the tin a little way into soft ground or sand.

4. Find different ways to play the tins as drums.

### Taking it forward

- Use really big catering tins as well as smaller household ones to create different sounds.

- Play them with the natural materials that you can find outdoors.

- Listen to the different sounds that heavy rain or pouring water will make on different sized tins.

### What's in it for the children?

The children get the opportunity to recycle in order to create some music. They can explore different types of sounds and the use of a range of natural materials.

# ainting on a plastic sheet

## What you need:

- Plastic builder's sheeting
- Duct tape
- Paint
- A variety of brushes and rollers

## What to do:

1. Wrap the builder's plastic around any static structure, such as a climbing frame or stretch it between two permanent objects.
2. Secure the plastic well with duct tape.
3. Use the variety of different utensils to paint!

### ing it forward

Get the children to stand on both sides of the plastic and mirror painting with each other.

Paint in the rain and watch how the raindrops settle on the plastic and cause the paint to mix.

Take prints from your plastic painting by pressing a sheet of paper over the top while it is still wet.

### at's in it for the children?

children get the opportunity
engage in some large scale
nting which is not only good for
eloping their artistic talents but
for their balance, hand eye
rdination and proprioception.

# Small world stations

## What you need:

- Small containers such as planters, raised beds or tyres
- A variety of textures such as sand, gravel, bark, soil, grass
- Small world figures

## What to do:

1. Fill a number of containers with different textures

2. Encourage the children to create real habitats that correspond to their small world play.

**Taking it forward**

- Enlarge the small world play spaces that you created outdoors to allow more children to engage.

- Provide opportunities for the children to introduce other elements into their play like water.

- Change the textures available to respond to the children's interests.

## What's in it for the children?

Small world is a really important element of Early Years education. It is crucial in developing a range of skills including speech, language, imagination and social skills. The significant difference between small world play indoors and out is that in outdoor play you can create real habitats with natural materials which gives the play a whole other dimension.

# Mud paint

## What you need:

- Soil
- Paint pots or beakers
- Water
- Food colouring
- Card for painting on

## What to do:

1. Put your soil into paint pots or beakers to make mixing easier.
2. If you want smooth paint pick out any stones or lumps.
3. Slowly add water and stir until creamy (you can use the mixture just like this if you wish).
4. Add some drops of food colouring to your mud (you will see the difference in colour when you paint with it).

### Taking it forward

- Use your 'smooth' mud as you would use normal paint.
- Try 'dolloping' your textured mud onto cardboard to create mud piles.
- Pour your mud paint over other objects such as bits of egg box to produce a 3D mud picture.

### What's in it for the children?

Alongside all of the language and texture development, this is a lovely activity for encouraging children to be creative with the natural materials they have around them to create art.

# ebble pictures

## What you need:

- A variety of different sized and textured pebbles and stones
- Pillowcase or paving stone (optional)
- Camera (optional)

## What to do:

1. Give the children time to really examine the pebbles and stones.

2. Encourage the children to use the pebbles and stones to create a picture or pattern outside.

3. Use a pillowcase or paving stone to give the children a 'frame' to work within.

4. Get the children to photograph their work when it is finished.

### ng it forward

Make large pictures and patterns outside involving a number of children working together.

Add other natural materials such as sticks, leaves and flowers to your pebble art.

Try creating your pebble pictures n wet concrete for a more permanent reminder.

### t's in it for the children?

children are using natural erials to create art. There are of opportunities for talk and ussion about the artwork that are making as well as the ure, shape and size of the oles and stones that they are g.

# Stick painting

## What you need:

- Large and small sticks
- A variety of paint brushes and sponges
- Paint

## What to do:

1. Ask the children to collect sticks and twigs in a range of sizes.
2. Get the children to look carefully at the sticks tha they collect, picking out any interesting features such as knobbles, bark texture, holes, splits and breaks.
3. Only paint the features that the children have identified leaving the rest of the stick unpainted.

### Taking it forward

- Try basing the colours and patterns that the children paint on the stick on patterns that they find in the outdoor environment like spots on a ladybird, stripes on a wasp, lines in the bark of a tree or veins on a leaf.

### What's in it for the children?

This activity gives the children the opportunity to look closely at natural objects within their environment. There are lots of opportunities for discussion not only about colour, texture and shape but also about why the sticks look the way they do and what has caused their interesting features.

# Stinging nettle tea

## What you need:

- **Rubber gloves** (for nettle picking)
- **12 fresh stinging nettle leaves**
- **Tea pot**
- **Boiling water**
- **Tea strainer**
- **Sugar or sweetener** (if required)

## What to do:

1. Use rubber gloves to pick your nettles.
2. Put the leaves into the tea pot and add boiling water.
3. Leave to infuse for three or four minutes.
4. Pour the liquid through a strainer into a cup.
5. Let the children taste the tea, making sure it is not too hot.

**Taking it forward**

You could also try using other commercial berry or herb teas to taste.

**What's in it for the children?**

The children have the opportunity to investigate the properties of various plants that grow in the outdoors.

# Weaving twig collector

## What you need:

- **Sticks or twigs** (one approximately 20cm to 30cm long and one approximately 10cm)
- **Heavy duty tape**
- **String, wool, twine or strips of fabric**

## What to do:

**1.** Use tape to attach two of the sticks together to make a 'Y' shape (if you can find a 'Y' shaped sti so much the better).

**2.** Cover the bottom of your 'Y' shape with string, wool, twine or fabric. This will make the handle o your collector.

**3.** Attach a piece of string, wool, twine or fabric securely just above the handle to one of the stick

**4.** Weave backwards and forwards between the two sticks in a zig zag until you get to the top.

**5.** Secure your string, wool, twine or fabric by tying, gluing or taping it.

**6.** When you are out looking for 'fairy finds' or natur materials, thread what you discover in between tl strings to keep it in place.

### Taking it forward

- Fill the collecting twigs with seasonal flora and fauna and display them around your setting.
- Use a much bigger 'Y' shaped twig.
- Try weaving directly into a tree or shrub (depending on the size).

### What's in it for the children?

This is a great activity for fine motor development and also gives the children an unusual way of making their own personal collection of natural things.

# ʳuddle painting

## What you need:

- Vegetable oil
- Food colouring
- Small containers
- A shallow puddle
- Paper
- Teaspoon

## What to do:

1. Mix a small amount of vegetable oil with a few drops of food colouring in a small container and stir vigorously.

2. Repeat with other colours until you have got the number of colours that you require.

3. Spoon some of each oil and colour mixture onto the surface of a shallow puddle.

4. Float your paper on top of the puddle until you can begin to see the oil showing through.

5. Lift the paper from one corner and leave to dry.

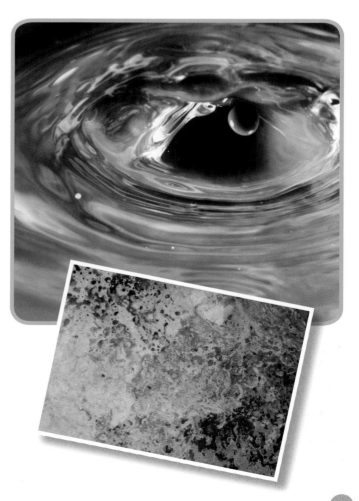

### ʳking it forward

As well as using puddles, try this effect on a wet paving stone.

Use different thicknesses and colours of paper (the thicker the paper the better the effect).

Try the effect without the oil and then without the paint. What happens and why?

### ʳat's in it for the children?

ʳere is lots of science as well as ʳ involved in this activity. The ʳdren will be able to see how the ʳour gets trapped inside the oil ʳ how the oil floats on top of the ʳer allowing it to be picked up by ʳ paper.

ʳantastic Ideas for Creativity Outdoors

19

# Eggshell painting

## What you need:

- Eggshells
- Paint
- Glue

## What to do:

1. Wash your eggshells.
2. Paint them on the outside while they are still in large pieces.
3. Allow the children to break up the painted eggshells into smaller pieces.
4. Use the pieces to create and enhance their artwork outdoors.

**FOOD allergy !**

### Taking it forward

- Colour the eggshells by boiling them with onion skins or other natural materials rather than painting them.
- Get the children to match the colours that they paint the shells in response to what they can see in their outdoor environment.

### What's in it for the children?

The children will be experiencing a natural material in a different way to create art. There is lots of opportunity to talk about colour, texture and how the children are using this material in their work.

# Collecting jars

## What you need:

- **Plastic storage jars** (various sizes)
- **Pipe cleaners**
- **Beads**
- **Fabric**
- **Wool**

## What to do:

1. Wrap a pipe cleaner around the neck of the jar.
2. Join two or three pipe cleaners together to make a handle.
3. Thread beads onto the pipe cleaner handle.
4. Tie pieces of fabric and wool in between the beads.
5. Twist the ends of your handle around the pipe cleaner at the neck of the jar.
6. For a more natural looking collection jar, wrap bunches of raffia around the neck of your jar and fill with the various natural materials you can find, labelling them as you go along.

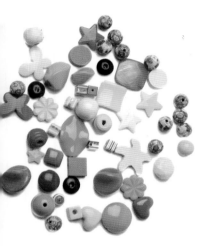

### Taking it forward

Try using natural materials like conkers, pieces of wood, pine cones or beech nuts instead of beads. Some of these will need to be pre-drilled to create the hole for threading. Use grasses or leaves instead of the wool and fabric.

### What's in it for the children?

The children are creating their own collecting jar for all of their outdoor discoveries. The jars can be used for a range of activities from mini beast hunting to collecting natural resources for a piece of transient art.

Fantastic Ideas for Creativity Outdoors

# Den building

- Large sticks
- Twigs
- String, twine or wool
- Pegs
- Fabric

## What to do:

1. Use large sticks and twigs to create an outer structure.
2. Secure the structure with string, twine or wool.
3. Cover and enhance it with smaller sticks and/ or fabric.
4. Secure with pegs.

## Taking it forward

- Try making a group den on a much larger scale.
- Give the children a den challenge like making it waterproof or windproof.
- See who can make the tallest or smallest den.
- Create dens for fictional characters such as fairies and elves.

## What's in it for the children?

The children will have to think a lot about what is going to make a good den. They will have lots of opportunity to practise their skills of perseverance and re-building. As a group activity, den making usually facilitates lots of discussion as children need to work together to achieve success.

# Hammer art

## What you need:

- Selection of flowers, leaves and grasses
- Blotting paper
- Kitchen roll
- Hammer or small rubber mallet

### Health & Safety
Make sure that children are supervised and that their fingers are well out of the way when using the hammer.

## What to do:

1. Collect the natural items that you want to make your artwork with.

2. Lay them out on your blotting paper in a picture or pattern.

3. Cover with the kitchen paper.

4. Gently hammer the kitchen paper until the outline of your objects begin to appear through it.

5. Remove the layer of kitchen paper, peel off your flowers and leaves and there will be an imprint of these underneath on your blotting paper.

## Taking it forward

- Try doing this on a much larger scale with larger leaves or flowers.
- Make a number of small pieces of hammer art and attach them together to make a paper patchwork quilt.

## What's in it for the children?

The children are getting the opportunity to discover more about how plants are made and how their leaves and flowers are made up of moisture and colour pigments as well as understanding one of the ways that prints can be created.

# Colour match and mix

## What you need:

- **Paint shade cards** (from DIY store)
- **Laminator**
- **Hole punch**
- **Treasury tags or split pins**

## What to do:

1. Sort the shade cards into colour groups or a mixed collection.
2. Laminate the individual cards.
3. Punch a hole into the top left hand corner of each card.
4. Join the cards together with a treasury tag or split pin.
5. Let the children take their shade cards into the outdoor environment and match them to the objects that they find.

### king it forward

Set up an outdoor paint mixing station so that when the children have identified one of the colours on their cards in an object outdoors they can then have a go at mixing that shade to paint a picture of the object.

### at's in it for the children?

s activity not only encourages children to look closely at the ironment but it also introduces m to the concepts of shades ranges of colour. If you set up paint station, it also creates an portunity to explore colour mixing a purpose.

# Nature frame

## What you need:

- Cardboard (A4 size)
- Ruler
- Scissors
- Lollipop stick
- Sellotape or glue

## What to do:

1. Draw a straight line, 4cm from each edge of your card. The lines should be the full width and lengt of the card.

2. Once all four lines have been drawn cut out the rectangle that you have created in the middle.

3. You should now have created a cardboard frame

4. Attach the lollipop stick as a handle to the bottor of your frame with sticky tape or glue.

5. Children hold the lollipop stick handle and then look through the frame to spot interesting natural features.

### Taking it forward

- Provide digital cameras to see if the children can then take a photograph of the things they have identified in their frame.

- Set up an art or workshop station so that the children can make or draw what they have 'framed'.

- Create 'cloud spotting' frames for the children to use to look for shapes within clouds.

### What's in it for the children?

This activity encourages the children to look more closely at their surroundings and identify interesting colours, shapes and textures. Having the portable frame really helps them to zoom in and out on what they are looking at.

## What you need:

- 1 cup of used coffee grounds
- ½ cup of cold coffee
- 1½ cups of flour
- ½ cup of salt
- Mixing bowl

## What to do:

1. Measure out all of the ingredients into a bowl.

2. Start with only one cup of the flour and add more if the dough is too sticky to work with.

3. Knead the dough together with your hands, then roll it into small balls, about the size of your palm.

4. Now flatten the round balls using the palm of your hand.

5. Press natural materials like leaves, shells, twigs and stones into the dough and then remove them carefully.

6. Allow the dough to dry overnight.

### ing it forward

Try replacing the coffee grounds with sand or soil for different textures and colour or take them out altogether for a very natural appearance.

### at's in it for the children?

children have first hand erience of seeing how materials their properties can change. re are lots of opportunities for guage development through loration of texture.

# Tree faces

## What you need:

- Clay
- A selection of natural materials
- Mirrors to observe their appearance
- Trees or walls to work on

## What to do:

1. Ask the children to mould a piece of clay into a ball about the size of a tennis ball.

2. Instruct the children to flatten the ball between their hands until it becomes a rough circle.

3. Press the circle into the bark of a tree or wall.

4. Ask the children to use natural materials to make a representation of their face.

### Handy hint

If you are using clay with young children work the pieces first before you let them have a go.

### Taking it forward

- Try using dough instead of clay as it is easier to manipulate but it's not as sticky. If you add some texture to the dough like sand, soil or coffee grounds, it will help it to stick a little better.

### What's in it for the children?

The children have the opportunity to name all of their facial features. They will be developing their skills of transference and representation as they select natural objects to mimic their features.

# rinting on eggs

## What you need:

- Leaves, ferns, grasses and flowers
- Uncooked eggs in their shells
- A pair of tights
- The skin of 10 brown onions
- Stainless steel pan
- 4 ½ cups of water
- 2 tablespoons of white vinegar
- Sieve
- Slotted spoon

## What to do:

1. Lay the leaf or flower over the egg.
2. Put the egg into the foot of a pair of tights and tie a knot so that the leaf or flower is held tight against the egg.
3. Put the onion skins into the pan.
4. Add the water and the vinegar.
5. Bring to the boil and simmer for 20 minutes.
6. Strain the onion skins, making sure you keep the water!
7. Make sure the eggs are at room temperature before you put them into the onion dye so they don't crack.
8. Put your eggs into the water and simmer for up to 20 minutes.
9. Lift out with a slotted spoon leave to cool and see the resulting patterns on the egg.

*Health & Safety*

Boiling the water and simmering the eggs is an adult only activity.

**king it forward**

Try dying your eggs with different natural substances like grass, moss, fruit or bark.

**at's in it for the children?**

e children have the opportunity follow instructions, observe a cess taking place and also see manent change to an object by lying heat.

# Ice art

## What you need:

- **Water**
- **Circular containers** (various sizes)
- **Natural materials** – berries, leaves, flowers, petals, bark, fruit, seeds etc.
- **String**

## What to do:

1. Pour about 2cm of water into the bottom of the container.
2. Place your natural materials in the water.
3. Place a loop of string into the container so one e is in the water and the other end hangs over the outside of the container.
4. Freeze over night (or during the winter leave outside).
5. Hang from the branches of trees as fairy art.

### Taking it forward

- Try freezing disks of ice without adding any natural materials. When the ice has set, drop rock salt and food colouring onto it before releasing it from the container for a unique effect.

### What's in it for the children?

The children have first hand experience of the materials and their changing properties. The texture of the natural materials, water and ice all provide opportunities for language development and discussion.

# Newspaper sculpture

## What you need:
- Newspapers
- Masking tape

## What to do:
**1.** Flatten your newspaper out.

**2.** Taking the longest side make a tight newspaper roll.

**3.** Secure with masking tape.

**4.** Repeat until you have lots of newspaper rolls.

**5.** Attach together using masking tape to make gigantic sculptures outside.

**Taking it forward**
- Try enhancing your structures with natural materials such as twigs and leaves.
- Make some miniature rolls and try creating mini sculptures.

**What's in it for the children?**

The children will be learning a lot about how to build structures that can stand and support their own weight. It is also a great opportunity to get children to explore scale and build on a much larger scale than they would normally do in an indoor environment.

# Sun prints

## What you need:

- Range of natural resources
- Sun print (photo-sensitive) paper
- Some sun!

## What to do:

1. Collect a variety of small natural objects like leaves, twigs and feathers. The more interesting their outline shape the more effective the final work will be.

2. Lay your objects onto the sun print paper.

3. Leave in a sunny spot outdoors for a few minutes.

4. Remove your objects and see the patterns they have made.

**Health & Safety**

Consideration should be given to the possible risk of splinters and use of sharp objects.

king it forward

Draw round some of the objects first to give the children an idea about how their outlines will look. This will help them to choose which objects they might use.

Create pictures and patterns with the natural objects on your sun paper.

hat's in it for the children?

s activity gives a very speedy perience of how materials and our can react when subjected to sun. The children will also have opportunity to consider pattern, pe and texture as they make ir selection of materials.

antastic Ideas for Creativity Outdoors

# Flying tubes

## What you need:

- A4 sheet of thin card
- Lots of paper clips
- Sellotape

## What to do:

1. Curl the card onto itself to form a cylinder.
2. Secure with a paper clip at each end.
3. Seal the seam along the side of the cylinder with Sellotape.
4. Put paperclips next to each other around the perimeter of one of the ends of the cylinder.
5. Once all of the paperclips are in place children can toss their tube in the air and watch it fly.

### Taking it forward

- This activity can be scaled up or scaled down depending on the space that you have got available and the number of paper clips you have got to hand!

- If you create a tube using an A1 size piece of card then you could use wooden clothes pegs instead of paper clips.

### What's in it for the children?

Not only will the children be learning about how weight can affect an object in flight they will also be engaging in a very physical activity which will help to develop their gross and fine motor skills alongside their physical dexterity.

# Bouncing ball

## What you need:

- Warm water
- Borax
- Food colouring
- 2 paper cups
- PVA glue
- Cornflour
- Lollipop stick

## What to do:

1. Put two tablespoons of water, half a teaspoon of Borax powder and a few drops of food colouring into one of the paper cups.

2. Stir until the powder is dissolved.

3. Pour one tablespoon of glue into the other paper cup.

4. Add one tablespoon of cornflour to the glue (do not stir).

5. Next add half a teaspoon of the Borax solution from the other cup to the glue mixture (do not stir).

6. Leave to sit for 15 seconds and then stir.

7. When the mixture becomes too stiff to stir take it out of the pot and roll it in your hands.

8. The mixture will continue to stiffen as you roll it.

9. Once it is hard enough, bounce!

### Health & Safety

Please ensure children are not tempted to try the solution as Borax can be harmful if consumed in large quantities.

### king it forward

Try making gigantic bouncy balls by increasing the amount of mixture that you use.

Change the colour of the balls by changing the colour of food colouring you use.

Add glitter to the mixture for a bit of sparkle.

### at's in it for the children?

e children are getting the portunity to see how materials  change their properties en other materials are added them. The bounciness of the s themselves will promote lots arge scale physical activity doors.

# No burst bubbles

## What you need:

- 1 cup of cooled boiled water
- 1 tablespoon of washing up liquid
- 1 teaspoon of glycerine
- Something to blow your bubbles with e.g a straw

## What to do:

1. Mix all of the ingredients together.
2. Let them sit for 24 hours.
3. Stir gently and then get blowing outdoors in the wind!

### Taking it forward

- Experiment with the sizes and shapes of bubble blowers that you make and see if this effects the bubbles poppability.

### What's in it for the children?

There is a real element of experimentation to both the creation and the using of this activity with lost of opportunities for the children to try different things. There are also lots of outdoor physical games that you can get the children playing which involve bubbles.

# Playground paint

## What you need:

- 1 cup of cornflour
- 1 cup of water
- Small pots or muffin tin tray
- Food colouring

## What to do:

1. Mix the cornflour with the water and stir.
2. Transfer the mixture into the small pots or muffin tins.
3. Add food colouring until you get the desired intensity of colour.
4. Paint directly onto the playground with a variety of brushes, sponges or other materials.

### Taking it forward

Try colouring your playground paint with other substances like powder paint or natural dye (see onion activity on page 29).

Use this paint on other surfaces such as tree bark.

### What's in it for the children?

The children get to mix their own paint, which will often inspire them then to use it. They will also have the opportunity to experience painting on surfaces with different textures, which may require them to manipulate their painting tools in different ways.

Fantastic Ideas for Creativity Outdoors

# Water spray pictures

## What you need:

- An old shower curtain or large sheet of paper
- Paint or food colouring
- Spray bottles
- Water

## What to do:

1. Attach the shower curtain or paper to a vertical surface such as a wall, tree or fence.
2. Mix your paint to a runny solution or add food colouring to water.
3. Pour your mixture into spray bottles.
4. Aim your bottle towards your painting surface and spray!

Taking it forward

- Vary the intensity of the colour by adding a higher concentration of paint or food colouring.
- Try spray painting onto other surfaces such as a tree bark or walls.

## What's in it for the children?

The spraying action itself is good for developing children's fine motor skills and there will also be opportunities to further develop their hand/eye coordination, balance and upper body strength. This activity is a good one for encouraging the children to explore colour mixing as well as talking about how the spray bottle squirts the paint.

# Sandy hands mosaic

## What you need:

- Damp sand or soil
- Small objects
- Plaster of Paris
- Zip lock freezer bag
- 1 wooden lollipop stick

## What to do:

1. Press your hand into damp sand or soil until it is about two inches deep.
2. Line your handprint with all of the small objects you have found.
3. Put plaster of Paris and water together in the freezer bag, following the instructions on the packet.
4. Squeeze the bag until the plaster is mixed.
5. Cut off the corner of the bag and squeeze the plaster into the handprint.
6. Use the lollipop stick to spread the plaster into the fingers and thumb.
7. Leave to set for 30 minutes.
8. Dig up and dust off the sand or soil.

### Taking it forward

- Try making impressions of other body parts or objects that you find.
- Push a lollipop stick into the base of your handprint while the plaster is still wet to give you something to hold it up with.

### What's in it for the children?

The children get the opportunity to experience texture as they make their handprints and also touch and feel the small objects that they are going to mosaic with. The plaster of Paris also changes its properties from powder to liquid to solid through the process of this activity, which creates lots of opportunities for talk and questioning.

# aby oil sun catchers

## What you need:

- Different-sized circles for drawing around
- Scissors
- Baby oil
- Small container
- Coloured paper
- Cotton buds
- String or ribbon for hanging

## What to do:

1. Draw around a selection of different-sized circles and cut them out.
2. Pour a small amount of oil into a container.
3. Take a cotton bud, dip it into the oil and use this to draw on the circular piece of paper.
4. Once the pattern is finished attach string or ribbon to the circle.
5. Hang outdoors in the sun.

king it forward

Use large pieces of paper and brushes for children who have less dexterity.

Fold your paper first to give some guidelines for children to follow.

Try using white paper and oil for a snowy effect.

at's in it for the children?

e children are employing a ge of skills in the production of ir sun catchers. Alongside all he fine motor skills involved in wing and cutting there are lots of portunity to think and talk about y the oil has changed the paper.

# Chalk dust hand prints

## What you need:

- Two people
- Playground chalk
- 1 lollipop stick
- Flat outdoor surface

## What to do:

1. One person lays their hand or hands flat on the surface they are going to be using.

2. A second person takes the playground chalk and the lollipop stick and rubs the stick up and down the side of the chalk to create dust.

3. Once the dust has covered the back of the flat hand/s and the area surrounding it, carefully lift the hand/s and see the pattern you have created

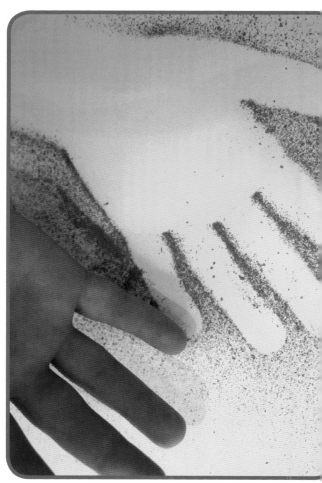

### Taking it forward

- Once you have mastered the skill then you can try it with other body parts or natural objects such as feathers, leaves or ferns.

- Try mixing different colours of chalk dust for different effects.

### What's in it for the children?

This idea was inspired by cave paintings. It would be interesting for the children to have a look at prehistoric cave man hand prints and see how our ancestors used their bodies to make art.

# olling stick art

## What you need:

- Large sticks or small logs
- Paint
- Paper

## What to do:

1. Put a generous amount of different colours of paint at different places on your stick.

2. Roll the stick backwards and forwards in all directions on your paper.

3. Add more paint as necessary.

### ing it forward

Vary the size of the log that you use.

Create a group piece of art with a large log.

Vary the texture of the surface that you work on under the paper as that will add to the pattern.

### at's in it for the children?

children are using their skills of d/eye coordination and fine and ss motor. They are also getting opportunity to explore texture then see how that texture can transferred into a pattern with use of paint.

# Build a fairy house

## What you need:

- Miniature accessories
- Moss
- Twigs
- Leaves
- Pebbles

## What to do:

1. Talk about where in your environment would make a good fairy house and why.

2. Use your natural materials to create your fairy house.

3. Make a miniature version of anything that you think the fairies might need using natural materials that you can find in your outdoor space

### king it forward

Use this as an introduction to the idea that fairies have come to live in your setting, in which case you get to spend many happy hours playing.

### at's in it for the children?

s of opportunities for the velopment of their talk and agination, to explore texture and evaluate which resources would ke effective building materials.

# Mud modelling

## What you need:

- Soil
- Water
- Sticks (for stirring)
- Natural materials for decoration

## What to do:

1. Mix the soil with a small amount of water to create thick mud.

2. Add more soil or water until your mud modelling material is of the right consistency.

3. Manipulate the mud to create a range of shapes.

4. Decorate your mud models with natural materials such as feathers, leaves, pebbles and fir cones.

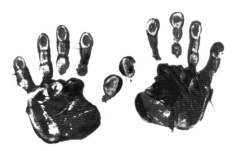

### Taking it forward

- Add other substances to your mud mix like sand or sawdust to change the texture.

- Make 'mud men' instead of snowmen.

- Hold a mud modelling outdoor exhibition.

### What's in it for the children?

The children are having the opportunity to experiment with texture and consistency. They will be able to experience the change in the properties of the soil as they add water and then use their fine and gross motor skills to manipulate the modelling material they have made into a piece of outdoor art.

# Painted paper tube sculpture

## What you need:

- Lots of cardboard tubes
- Kitchen towel
- Masking tape
- Paint
- Large tray
- Newspaper or packing paper

## What to do:

1. Cut your cardboard tube so it is slightly smaller than a sheet of kitchen towel.
2. Wrap your tube in a sheet of kitchen towel tucking in the ends.
3. Secure the kitchen towel inside the tube with a piece of masking tape at each end.
4. Squirt paint into the bottom of the tray.
5. Roll your tube backwards and forwards mixing the colours and creating patterns.
6. Stand your tube on its end to dry.
7. Once the tubes are dry, take sheets of newspaper and twist them together to create 'newspaper snakes'.
8. Thread the coloured tubes onto the newspaper.
9. Twist together to create a sculpture or leave in straight lines.

### ...king it forward

...Incorporate the newspaper and paper roll lengths into the natural environment weaving them through trees and bushes.

...Match the shades that you use in the tray to the ones that you can see in your outdoor space.

### ...at's in it for the children?

...ing this activity the children ...be experimenting with colour ...ing and then using their finished ...ations to create large scale ...ces of outdoor artwork.

# Drip painting

## What you need:

- Squeezy bottles
- Paint
- A tree or wall
- Sheets of paper

## What to do:

1. Fill the squeezy bottles with paint.
2. Squeeze them onto the bark of a tree to create a large drip.
3. Add other colours in different places.
4. Give the drips time to run (add more paint if needed).
5. Put the paper over a section of the drip painting and rub.
6. Peel back the paper to reveal your textured drip painting.

### Taking it forward

- Try drip painting on other surfaces like brick or glass.
- Draw a line of paint around the whole circumference of the tree and then repeat at different heights for a stripy effect.

### What's in it for the children?

This activity allows the children to experience how liquid moves over different surfaces. There are also lots of possibilities for exploring paint mixing as well as the technique of relief printing.

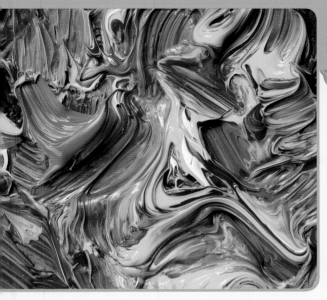

# Teasel and fir cone painting

## What you need:

- Paint
- PVA glue
- Fir cones
- Dried teasel heads
- Modelling clay or dough
- Lollipop sticks
- Materials for decoration such as beads, glitter, sequins, pulses and seeds

## What to do:

1. Mix your paint until it is about the thickness of double cream.
2. Add a spoonful of PVA glue to your paint and stir well.
3. Sit your fir cones and teasels onto a small piece of dough or clay to keep them steady while you paint them.
4. Use a lollipop stick to scoop up some of the paint and allow it to drip onto different parts of your teasel or fir cone.
5. Allow the paint to run into all of the cracks and crevices of your natural objects.
6. Decorate further if required.

**Taking it forward**

- Hang your teasels upside down by their stalks and paint them that way.
- Try using your teasels to apply paint to paper like a natural brush.
- Attach the finished creations to string or wool to create natural outdoor bunting.

**What's in it for the children?**

There is lots of opportunity to talk about texture in this activity, both in the consistency of the paint and the look and feel of the objects being painted. Children are also exploring a different method of painting by dripping rather than brushing the paint.

# endulum painting

## What you need:

- **Pipe cleaners**
- **Paper cups**
- **String**
- **Scissors**
- **Paint**
- **Paper** (optional)

## What to do:

1. Wrap one pipe cleaner around the neck of the paper cup and twist to secure.

2. Create a handle with a second pipe cleaner and attach to the first (your paper cup should now look like a small bucket).

3. Attach a length of string to the middle of your handle.

4. Puncture the bottom of the paper cup with the scissors *(adult activity)* to create a hole for the paint to escape from.

5. Half fill the cup with paint.

6. Swing the paint filled cup over your paper by holding the string.

### king it forward

Create a structure for your paint cups to hang from rather than holding them.

Try producing a huge pendulum picture by using a bucket instead of a paper cup.

Replace the paint with sand or salt for a different effect.

### hat's in it for the children?

ie children are experiencing how avity can help them to create t. If they are holding their paint endulum then they are using their hole body, balance and gross otor skills to create their art.

# Plunging

## What you need:

- **Plungers of various sizes**
- **Paint**
- **Paint trays**
- **Paper** (optional)

## What to do:

**1.** Dip the plungers into the paint.

**2.** Create patterns and pictures by printing on outdoor surfaces.

### Taking it forward

- Work on different surfaces, both horizontal and vertical.

- Try painting in pairs or groups and plunging in sequence.

- Create your plunger painting to music, making a print in time to the beat.

### What's in it for the children?

The children are creating art made purely from circles. This method of printing is very gross motor and involves hand eye coordination as well as upper body strength and balance.

# ashing line theatre

## What you need:

- **2 x 6ft washing lines**
- **2 cotton sheets**
- **Paint**
- **Felt tip pens**
- **Pegs**
- **Fabric** (lots of it)
- **Hats**

## What to do:

**1.** Tie your first washing line between two solid objects (for example trees).

**2.** Tie your second washing line about three feet in front of the first.

**3.** Paint and decorate one of your sheets and using the pegs, attach it to the first washing line as a backdrop.

**4.** Cut your second sheet in half and drape it over the second washing line for curtains.

**5.** Use any other fabric to wrap around the children for quick and easy costumes.

### ing it forward

Thread 1¼" binder clips onto the second washing line and clip your curtains to these. This will allow the curtains to open and close more smoothly.

f you haven't got fabric you can create your backdrop with lining paper or just use your natural surroundings.

### at's in it for the children?

s is a great opportunity for the dren to engage in open ended play. Because the setting is y to change it means that the dren can make it whatever y want it to be. You can also g in lots of other creative s by encouraging children to ate props and music for their duction.

# Make your own kite

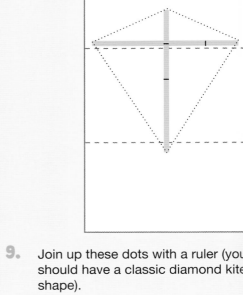

## What you need:

- **Scissors** (big enough to cut through the skewers)
- **2 x 30cm bamboo BBQ skewers**
- **Plenty of thin coloured plastic, in sheets or bags**
- **Sticky tape**
- **Light string, or polyester sewing thread**
- **A ruler**
- **A black marker pen**

## What to do:

1. Cut the pointed ends off the skewers *(adult activity)*.

2. On the first skewer mark exactly half way using your marker.

3. On the second skewer mark half way and then mark exactly half of that.

4. Flatten out your plastic bag or plastic sheets.

5. Divide your plastic bag or sheets into three sections.

6. Lay the first skewer horizontally across the bottom of the top third of your plastic.

7. Lay the second skewer vertically down the middle of your plastic so that one of the black marks nearest the end of this skewer is on top of the middle mark of the first skewer.

8. Draw dots at the ends of both skewers. Then put the skewers to one side.

9. Join up these dots with a ruler (you should have a classic diamond kite shape).

10. Cut out the diamond shape you have made.

11. Replace the skewers as before.

12. Before attaching the plastic to the ends of the skewers using sticky tape tie the skewers where they cross tightly together with string.

13. Attach your line and wait for wind!

## king it forward

Make the kites larger and smaller by changing the length of the sticks you use.

Attach a tail to your kite made from other recycled plastic.

Fly a number of kites at the same time and create 'art in the sky'. You can then capture your art on a photograph.

## What's in it for the children?

The children will be able to practice their skills of measuring and cutting as well as talking about their selection of colours and patterns.

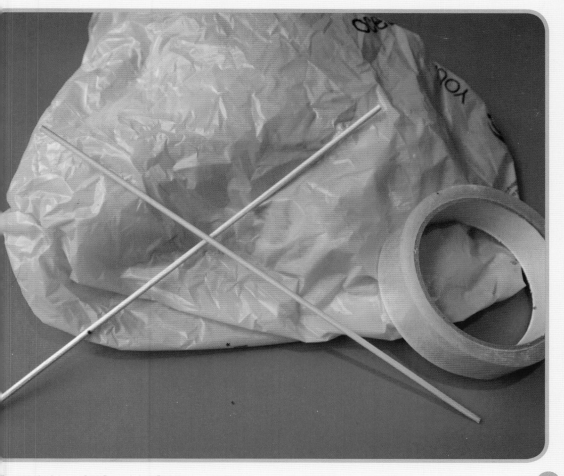

# Message pebbles

## What you need:

- Pebbles of different sizes
- Paint
- Magazines
- PVA glue

## What to do:

1. Wash and dry your pebbles.
2. Paint your pebbles (optional).
3. Cut letters and words in different styles out of magazines and newspapers.
4. Glue the letters and words to the pebbles.
5. When dry give the pebbles an extra few coats of PVA glue.
6. If they are going to be left outside varnish them fi
7. Leave messages for your friends.

### Taking it forward

- Put images and symbols onto your pebbles.
- Remember to make extra vowels and commonly used letters like 's'.

### What's in it for the children?

Not only do the children get another engaging way of communicating with each other they will also be developing their phonic skills in both the creating and reading of the messages.

## What you need:

- **Pipe cleaners**
- **Beads or natural objects**
- **Stick or twig approximately 30cm long**
- **String** (optional)
- **Tape** (optional)
- **Bubble mixture**

## What to do:

1. Take a pipe cleaner and thread a variety of beads or natural objects onto it (you may have to pre-drill some of the natural objects that you want the children to use).

2. Bend the two ends of the pipe cleaner around until they meet each other.

3. Twist the ends of the pipe cleaner together and then attach to the stick by twisting.

4. You may want to re-enforce the attachment to the stick by using tape or string.

5. Get the children to dip their beaded wands into bubble mixture and have fun blowing bubbles outdoors!

### king it forward

Make some large beaded bubble wands by joining pipe cleansers together or using stronger wire.

Try putting a beaded pipe cleaner at both ends of your stick for extra bubble blowing capacity.

### hat's in it for the children?

e children will have the portunity to experience pattern d texture as well as making cisions about design and lour. The threading of the beads natural objects is good for omoting fine motor development.

# Sticky viewing box

## What you need:

- **Cardboard box**
  (approximately 60cm by
  30cm – big enough for a
  child to get their head inside
  but not too big so that they
  can't hold it up)
- **Clear sticky backed plastic**
- Scissors
- Ruler

## What to do:

1. Cut one side out of the box completely.

2. On the other five sides cut out the middle of the
   side leaving a 'frame' of at least 3cm.

3. Inside the box put the sticky backed plastic acros
   the frames you have created making sure that yo
   are attaching it with the sticky side facing out!

4. Children use their box to collect natural objects a
   stick them onto the 'sticky windows' on the outsi
   of their box.

5. When they have collected something on all five
   windows they can put the box onto their head an
   look at their world in a very different way!

## king it forward

Create an outdoor art station and get the children to draw what they see.

Try this activity on a much bigger scale by using boxes that the children can walk into or sit in with a much larger sticky window.

## at's in it for the children?

e children are encouraged to look sely at their surroundings while y are making their collections. ere will be lots of opportunity to k about the colours and textures the natural objects that they find. en they are looking through ir sticky windows, it is a good ortunity to get the children to nk about pattern and shape as l as talk about how the world ks different.

# Natural frame

## What you need:

- 4 twigs
- Sticky tack or masking tape
- String, wool, twine or rafia
- Natural decorations
  (depending on the seasons)

## What to do:

1. If you are making a square frame choose twigs that are approximately the same length.
2. Lay your sticks out in the shape you want them to be first.
3. Put a small piece of sticky tack between the sticks where they meet or bind them with the tape.
4. Wrap your string repeatedly around the sticks where they meet.
5. Attach natural objects to the frame for decoration
6. Frame your fairy pictures, natural objects or writing.

### Taking it forward

- Suspend natural objects like acorns, pine cones, leaves etc. from the top of your frame. These frames look equally good hanging indoors or outside.

### What's in it for the children?

The children have the opportunity to develop their measuring skills and also shape recognition. Wrapping string around the corners can be quite a fiddly task and so is very good for their hand/eye coordination and fine motor skill development.